WHAT!!? NO APOCALYPSE?

—1000—

Angry crowds were yesterday demanding to know why they were still there. Furious at prophecies that said the world would come to an end on New Year's Day, AD1000, they took the law into their own hands and marched through the streets waving banners and shouting, "We want the end of the world to be nigh!"

Shake

In London, England, the official response was mixed.

"Off the record," said one cleric, "the Bible does mention an occurrence at the millennium. Something along the lines of 'Shake in thy clogs, this is the big one'. I think it's Revelations, but don't quote me."

Cover-up

Members of the action group "Apocalypse When?" are claiming there's been a **cover-up**. "We've been swindled!" said an AW spokes-peasant. "All we've heard for centuries is **'Watch it! The end of the world's coming! Best behave yourselves, lads.'** And now what happens? Absolutely nothing, that's what! It's a disgrace."

The "Apocalypse When?" office has been swamped with requests for information. "It's all been a plot to keep the workforce quiet," they insist. "All these years we've been meek and mild like the vicar told us, so we don't go to hell when the world ends. And for what? If you ask us, the establishment's in it up to the eyebrows."

Land

But it's not just the peasants who've been affected

There's more of this to do, now the world hasn't ended!

by Apocalypse fever. Wearing his AW sticker – "End not nigh? Ask me why!" – with pride, one distressed aristocrat moaned, "We've been ruined. Leases have been getting shorter for decades. On December 30 last year you couldn't rent anything for more than one day. It'll take ages for the market to recover."

Locked

Members of the All Soothsayers Brotherhood (ASB), who many hold responsible for the high level of expectation regarding the end of the world, were unavailable for comment. But we did manage to track down one seer, who spoke to us from behind an oak door with iron studs and ten locks.

"I'm beginning to think that we got the wrong millennium," admitted the shame-faced stargazer. "But look on the bright side. The weather's been bad lately, so there's every chance we're in the early stages of a spectacularly awful Apocalypse. My advice to the public is **Hang on to your tickets!**"

The Medieval Messenger

was written by
Fergus Fleming
designed by
Karen Tomlins
and edited by
Paul Dowswell

With thanks to Ruth Russell (design), Guy Smith (illustrations), and Christopher Smith (consultant).

STRIKE A LIGHT!

Dark Ages over – it's official!

—1001—

So we're not a bunch of uncivilized illiterate savages after all! Ever since the Roman Empire fell to pieces six hundred years ago, historians have branded us a continent of brainless half-wits. But now the snooty scholars are playing a different tune. According to them we're back on the cultural map – with a vengeance.

Egghead

"Written records have a lot to do to do with it," admits one egghead monk. "Previously there were very few. These days almost every monastery worth its salt has a library."

So how does it feel to be civilized? "Fantastic!" says candlestick maker Baldwin Tubalard. "I can visit my cousin in Aquitaine now, and have a more than fifty percent chance of coming back alive – now that's what I call progress!"

How the two ages compare

DARK AGE 500–1000	MEDIEVAL AGE 1000–1450
Huts	Reach-for-the-sky cathedrals
Stupidity	Brains
Not much culture	Illuminations coming out of our ears
No money	Barrel-loads of it
Little trade	More trade than you can shake a mast at
Few written records	Manuscripts 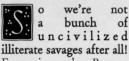

---

monks shamed
as hair ruse is rumbled

Bald Brother Etienne.

Monks who plugged their lifestyle as a cure for baldness are in court today for making false claims.

The trouble started when members of a French monastery lured thin-on-tops into their cloisters by promising to eliminate hair-loss problems. Novices soon found the "cure" was to have their heads shaved.

"I'd tried all the available treatments with no success," said Brother Etienne of Lyon. "When I heard of this offer it seemed too good to miss. Imagine my horror when I discovered I was going to be even balder than before."

But church leaders were quick to dismiss his claims. "This misguided individual is referring to the tonsure, a special trim in which the crown of the head is shaved as a gesture of humility. It so happens that this area of scalp also features in classic patterns of male baldness. The monasteries were quite within their rights to advertise it as a solution to hair-loss problems. Logically, if you're not meant to have any hair in that particular spot then its loss can't be a problem."

But the authorities are coming down on Etienne's side. A probe has been launched into monastery recruitment techniques. Meanwhile errant abbots are being advised to watch their step – **and their clippers.**

LET'S CALL IT RUSSIA!
KING VLAD IS NATION'S DAD!

—1003—

Vladimir, King of Kiev, has decided to form a new nation. Vlad is sick and tired of running a second-rate kingdom.

"World politics are going to change!" crowed the royal. "Nobody rated the Slavs in the past but now people are going to sit up and take notice. I'm going to build a superpower!"

Converted

Not half! Vlad has recently **married** his eighth wife, Princess Anna from Constantinople, and entered into an **alliance** with Anna's brother, Emperor Basil II. He's also **converted** himself and his subjects to Christianity, and has **conquered** pretty well everything immediately to the west of the Ural mountains.

New

The new state is to be called **Russia**. This comes from a Slav word *rus*, which is what the locals called **Vikings** who settled there in the eighth century. **And why not**?

"We're almost there. But our one big problem is writing," Vlad confided to the *Messenger*. "You lot in the West have it easy. You've got the Roman alphabet. Us? We've got the Cyrillic one."

Squashed

"Look at this – "Д," he ranted. "Know what that is? It's a D. Yes, a D. Hard to believe isn't it? Now look at this. Ф. It's an F. Looks more like a squashed butterfly to me."

Saddled

"We've been saddled with it since that Greek missionary Saint Cyril came here in the 850s to try to convert us to Christianity. He's lucky we didn't boil him alive and feed his remains to the wolves. Still, people will get used to it in a few more centuries."

ENGLAND CRUMBLES AS NORMANS CONQUER

Military analysts attribute the Norman victory to their cross-stitching and chain-stitching skills. Their hemming was also very accomplished.

WILL WALLOPS HAZZA

—— 1066 ——

Luck wasn't on England's side when they met the chain-mail-clad Norman heavies at Hastings. Anglo-Saxon frontliners had been expecting a quick victory over the visitors. Instead they were shredded as the Norman offensive tore gaping holes in their outer field.

Past it

"It was October, and we were past our best," said an English axeman. "We should have cut them to pieces. But we'd already had a heavy season, what with rebellions here and there, and an invasion by the Norwegians. By the time we got to Hastings we had already peaked."

The Normans' masterful fighting left the Saxons in disarray. An early casualty was King Harold, who was stretchered off with an arrow in the eye.

"It's tough on Hazza," said his opposite number King William. "But he spent too much time on summer campaigns. You can't expect to come out top if you don't concentrate on the games that really matter."

Big plans

King William, who has already hinted that his new subjects can call him 'The Conqueror', has big plans for England.

"First I'm going to build a large Tower in London," he said. "Then I'm going to see how much property people have got and then I'm going to tax them severely."

But first, William intends to commemorate his victory with a vivid depiction of his campaign against Harold. "We're calling it the Bayeux Tapestry," he told us. "Although between you and me, it's just a bit of embroidery."

RED TAPE RUNS WILD

'Twas the night before Domesday: Anxious aristocrats relish their pre-tax prosperity.

—— 1086 ——

Paperwork – who needs it? That's the message from angry English landowners as they struggle to meet the Domesday Book deadline.

"Nothing makes sense now that the Normans have taken over," moaned Lady Fotheringhay. Since her husband was killed at Hastings, Lady F. has single-handedly operated a farm in the village of Willybrook.

Fleece the rich

The Domesday Book is part of King William's new tax scheme to fleece the rich. Anyone who owns anything is being asked to fill in a questionnaire saying how many fields, houses, ducks, pigs, cows, sheep and servants they have. But for the weary Anglo aristocrats it's all too much.

Stumped

"I'm stumped," says Lady Fotheringhay. "Question Six asks whether my staff are freemen, bondservants, villeins, serfs or slaves. Well, really! How am I meant to know? **They all look the same to me.**"

ALL ABOARD THE INFIDEL EXPRESS!

Pope Urban says "Go for it!"

—1096—

The First Crusade is well underway having received official approval from the Pope. Lords from all over Western Europe are putting on their best helmets and heading for the Middle East. Their intention? To capture the holy city of Jerusalem and the holy land of Palestine, and teach the Muslim inhabitants (or *infidels*, as the crusaders call them) a lesson they'll never forget.

In the bag

The crusaders are doing well, thanks to a combination of their state-of-

Top notch gear gives our boys the edge.

Crusaders load up cargo boats in preparation for their three-year-long journey to Jerusalem.

the-art heavy cavalry and high-tech siege catapults.

"We've taken most major ports and are almost at Jerusalem," crowed breathless Belgian knight Fulk de Bulk. "I think we've got it in the bag."

Sacked

Not everyone's as happy as Fulk. Thousands of crusaders have died without getting anywhere near the Middle East. And thousands more have given up all hope of ever seeing Jerusalem. They've just sacked the nearest town beginning with J and gone home. **In fact some people are beginning to say it's all a waste of time.**

Sequel

Authorities are down-playing such suggestions. According to them the crusade has proved so popular that they are already planning several more.

"There is major sequel potential here," predicted Cardinal Goldwyn of Metro-Rome. "We foresee Second, Third and even Fourth Crusades. We've got a Children's Crusade in production and are looking at proposals for a People's Crusade. The public response has been tremendously enthusiastic."

The *Messenger* says: NOT IN THE MIDDLE EAST IT HASN'T!!

FRANK–LY CONFUSING

The Middle Easterners are calling crusaders "Franks". And the boys with crosses on their shirts are getting irritated.

"What a cheek! It's a bit over-familiar to be on first-name terms," says one indignant knight. "And if they must, why can't they get it right? Sure, lots of us are called Frank. But there are just as many who aren't. Some of us are Rons, some are Bills – I know at least five people called Bohemond – then there's Raymonds, Johns, Gregorys..."

Actually, says our linguistics correspondent, they call you *al-Faranj*. This sounds like "Franks" and is an Arabic word meaning *European*!

Next Week: IS YOUR BEST FRIEND AN INFIDEL?

CRUSADE SPECIAL ✠ CRUSADE SPECIAL

Crusading opportunities

Jousting and jabbing and slicing and slashing – just four of the treats in store on our crusades!

CHILDREN'S CRUSADE

Are you between 8 and 12 with nothing to do this summer? Then join the Children's Crusade! Along our scenic route to the holy land of Palestine you will see new wildlife, camp out in strange places, and learn the ins and outs of foreign woodcraft.

Give us **your** time, and in return we guarantee that **you will almost certainly never return alive!**

HERMITS' CRUSADE

Are you completely alone? Then join our crusade for the solitary gentleman. Travel without equipment, food or friends, and you will find many lovely spots in which to admire the tranquillity of the world. We particularly recommend the fine catacombs of the Middle East, in which you can be assured of eternal peace. Write enclosing stamped addressed parchment to

GOTCHA RECRUITMENT.

PETS' CRUSADE

Are you a pet? No, of course you're not – but you've probably got one or two. These little morsels can feel lonely when you're away fighting. So why not sign them up to our special Pets' Crusade? Call ARMY DINNERS now!

VILLAGE IDIOTS' CRUSADE

Are you an idiot? Yes? Then don't be ashamed to say so. Every village has one. **But here's your chance to look clever.** We're offering crusades at such cut-price rates they'll make your eyes cross!

PEOPLE'S CRUSADE

Are you a person? Yes? Then we want YOU to join our People's Crusade. No chain-mail, no horse, no chivalry. Just the gut determination to get a job done. You may not be able to do it, but who cares. All we want is people who are willing to try. Apply to NO FUTURE Enterprises.

JERUSALEM FALLS AS ARMY THUGS GO ON RAMPAGE

—— 1099 ——

Jerusalem has seen all kinds of visitors over the centuries. But none have been as ill-mannered as the crusaders. Having failed to pre-book, the mail-shirted louts simply turned up at the gate and demanded to be let in. When refused entry they took matters into their own hands and captured the town.

"We told them we were out of space, but they weren't taking No for an answer," said one dazed rep from the Jerusalem Tourist Board. "They just ran wild. I've never seen anything like it. The damage is enormous."

Trashed

"It is not a very good advertisement for Western civilization," agrees Adad Nirari, whose ten-room hotel, The Happy Haven, has been trashed from top to bottom. "I know we are supposed to have a tradition of hospitality, but this is going too far."

"Jerusalem is a holy city. Yet they strut around as if they own the place. They treat us Muslims like savages, whereas we're actually more civilized than they are. When they go back home they'll be taking our luxury goods like silks and spices with them, not to mention our ideas about medicine, astronomy and castle-building."

List

Angry Jerusalem hoteliers have drawn up a list of complaints against their uninvited conquerors. These include:
- **Breaking** down city walls
- **Storming** ramparts at all hours and **looting**
- Wholesale **slaughter** of Muslim and Jewish citizens
- Wading knee deep through **blood** of enemies.

But crusader chiefs were unrepentant. "Admittedly, the boys were tired after a long campaign," said one crusader knight. "They've been on the road for three long years.

Now we've achieved our aim of capturing the holy city of Jerusalem we feel like letting off steam.

"However the locals will be pleased to hear that most of us will soon be going home. But a few of us are going to stay to set up a crusader kingdom here, with a king."

Crusader chiefs have confirmed this story and look set to announce that Baldwin, brother of crusader leader Geoffrey de Bouillon, is in line for the top job.

Crusaders letting off some steam in Jerusalem.

Spot the enemy in your midst with our 4-page pull-out special.

BECKET KICKS BUCKET

KING'S CURSES CAUSE CALAMITY AT CANTERBURY

Thomas à Becket uttering his last words. ("Aaaaaaaagh," according to most witnesses.)

—— 1170 ——

Thomas à Becket, the merchant's son from Merton, England, who became chancellor to King Henry II, and rose to even greater fame as archbishop of Canterbury, has been struck dead by four of the King's knights.

Serf-razing power

As chancellor, Becket, 52, had been a leading figure in Henry II's campaign to give more power to the monarchy and less to the church. A trusted adviser to the King, Becket also excelled himself as a soldier, razing castles to the ground and leading troops.

But things turned sour when Henry appointed his pal to the top job in the English church – archbishop of Canterbury. Becket immediately changed character, championing the church and its right to remain free from royal interference.

Henry raged and ranted as Thomas:
• Opposed the raising of taxes on the church.
• Banished some of Henry's top men from church premises.
• Upheld the right of villainous churchmen to be tried by their own soft-on-crime church courts, rather than by the King's flogging-and-hanging style government courts.

Henry launched a no-holds-barred campaign to ruin his former friend, and Becket fled to France, fearing for his life. But Henry agreed to allow him to come home when Becket, backed by the Pope, threatened the King with a no-excuses, no-money-back, one-way ticket to hell!

Bad temper

Becket returned to Canterbury in December 1170, but his quarrel with Henry was far from over. When he banished more of Henry's top men from church, the King snapped. Cursing and snarling, he let it be known that Thomas à Becket was obviously **tired of living**. So four of the King's knights sped down to Canterbury and slew him in his own cathedral.

But news of his death has made Canterbury a shrine to his followers, and already there are reports that Becket is to be made a saint. Henry, meanwhile, is overcome with remorse and plans to seek forgiveness from the Pope himself.

"GET OUT OF MY HEAD!"

keyhole surgeon faces lockup

—— 1179 ——

Keyhole surgery? Angry patient Eldred Turnip is giving surgeons the length of his tongue. Having checked in for a trepanning operation – a routine procedure which involves drilling a hole in the skull to relieve headaches or bouts of madness – he came out with a gaping cavity the size of a saucer.

Latest thing

"They told me keyhole surgery was the latest thing," he told the *Messenger*. "But frankly I may as well have had it done by the local gravedigger. I mean, look at it."

Turnip is calling for revenge. "Six years in a dank dungeon would do," he told us.

Unfortunately for Eldred, although seers and sages predict that keys and keyholes will get smaller in the future, they're still extremely large and rather clumsy devices. Medical experts say Eldred should have avoided new-fangled hands-on surgery and stuck to the tried and trusted route of medicines and magic charms.

Mallet

"These so-called surgeons are just jumped-up barbers, or battlefield medics," said top physician Lancelot de Lozenge, "and expecting them to perform intricate operations is like asking a road-builder to fix your delicate gold bracelet with a great big mallet. Medicine has so much to offer I can't understand why Eldred took such drastic action."

Hands-on

Lozenge went on to tell the *Messenger*, "Therapeutic flowers and plants are available in great numbers, as are such health-giving foods as sugar and treacle. Why fix a bad head with painful surgery when a lotion of ginger and cinnamon will do the trick with much less fuss? Best of all, get yourself touched by someone with healing powers. Kings are best, if you can get near enough to beg them to touch you, but a Jew or Muslim who has converted to Christianity also has the ability to cure all sorts of maladies by simply laying their hands on the patient."

Wrong signs

"Besides, these surgeons often perform their grisly chores at completely inappropriate times of the year. Anyone connected with medicine knows that you can only treat particular ailments at set astrological moments. I, for example, would only tend to a patient with bad headaches when the Moon is rising in Sagittarius. It's just asking for trouble to do it at any other time."

Trepanning – top treatment for headaches. Don't try this at home, kids!

PARISIANS UPSET AS KING PAVES STREETS

—— 1185 ——

Older residents are up in arms as Paris becomes Europe's first city to have paved streets. Ever since cobble-laying started last year, citizens have feared for their heritage. Now matters have come to a head.

"It makes my blood boil," says refuse collector Pierre Stinque. "Medieval cities are meant to be poky mazes, knee-deep in filth and so gloomy you can't see your nose in front of your face. Why do we have to be different from everyone else? It'll ruin the tourist trade for starters."

King Philip, the man behind the project, got hot and bothered when we asked him how this change would affect the leisure industry.

"What leisure?" he snarled. "We don't have any. We work hard here. Show me a holidaymaker and I'll show you a head on a stick. We need business. And business needs good streets."

Despite the promise of increased trade, locals are still unhappy.

"It won't stop here," says Pierre. "Paved streets are just the beginning. Before you know it there'll be boulevards everywhere letting in sunlight, vapours and God knows what. The people won't stand for it. One day there'll be a revolution. You mark my words."

Street cobblers in action. Local maidens have been advised to steer well clear of these lewd and outspoken workers, who are renowned for their baggy tights and all too visible bottoms.

"KING CARNAGE" DIES IN TENT

Genghis sparks bloodbath horror

1227

The mighty Mongol Empire is bidding a tearful farewell to cut-throat killing machine Genghis Khan. The warlord, who tamed the Asian continent and still wanted more, has died.

Genghis, whose byword was "Join our horde and you'll never be bored", passed away in his tent *Dunpillagin'* pitched in the foothills of the Linbanshan mountains in China. His demise follows a long struggle against severe internal injuries. "He'd not been the same since he fell off his horse," said a royal insider.

He is best remembered for conquering half the world and annihilating anyone who stood in his way.

Massacre

As news of his death spread through the empire, tributes· poured in. "He certainly knew how to lay on a massacre," said a rival royal. "When it came to carnage, Genghis was king."

Jog Ogudei, landlord of the Rack & Ruin, Genghis's local tavern, said, "Some people say he was too tough. But sometimes you've got to be cruel to be kind. Those cities he razed – don't forget he gave those people the chance to surrender. You can't blame him for slaughtering them if they didn't take up his offer."

Put to sword

Genghis's body is currently being returned for burial at his headquarters in the Mongol capital of Karakorum.

The phrase "Put them to the sword" was never far from his lips, and soldiers in his funeral procession are making a special effort to show their respect by slaughtering anyone unfortunate enough to cross their path. "It's what he would have wanted," said a member of his entourage.

Ghenghis's glory days – against Prester John in "the greatest battle that ever was seen".

Rotten to the core... Is Genghis history's baddest apple?

The Mongols may have liked him, but no one else did. Some people even say Genghis was **worse** than fifth-century Slav madman Attila the Hun. So exactly who is the Baron of Barbarity, and Earl of Extermination?

Here on the *Messenger* we've compiled our own chart to answer that eternal question:

"Who is the baddest of the bad?"

Each category is awarded badness points from 1 to 10.

Messenger Messenger on the wall, Who's the BADDEST of them all?	GENGHIS KHAN	POINTS OUT OF 10	ATTILA THE HUN	POINTS OUT OF 10
Nickname	"Conqueror of the world"	6	"Scourge of God"	10
Appearance	Gangly, feline, long beard. Not particularly filthy.	4	Squat, scar-faced psychopath. Sinister moustache. Pointy hat. Absolutely filthy.	10
Character	Prone to acts of unspeakable violence. Cunning.	10	Cunning. Prone to acts of unspeakable violence.	10
Most barbaric exploits	Conquered half known world. Massacred entire cities. Used captives as human shields for army. Boiled enemy chiefs alive. Left mountain of human bones.	40*	Terrorized western Europe. Laid waste eastern Europe. Murdered brother. Invaded France because king refused to let him marry sister.	7
What his enemies said about him	He was sent by Satan to herald the end of the world.	10	He was sent by God to punish the world for its sins.	7
How he died	Long illness, following fall from horse.	0	Said to have been murdered in bed by his wife Ildeco.	10
TOTAL BADNESS POINTS	Congratulations, Genghis, the horse-loving nomad from the howling wastes of central Asia. You are HISTORY'S TOP TYRANT!	70	Bad luck, Attila, you may have had the looks, you may even have had the table manners, but when it comes to sheer IN-YOUR-FACE BARBARITY you're second rate, mate.	54

*****Messenger** staff felt 10 points was insufficient for this category.

NO WAR IS COMPLETE WITHOUT

ELKHORN'S

SAFETY VISORS

How often have you had your nose chopped off and thought, "I could have avoided that if only I'd been wearing a decent visor."? Probably scores of times.

Elkhorn's Safety Visors come to the rescue. Buy from us and you'll never suffer that embarrassing problem again.

Elkhorn completes your all-over metal body protection. Our helmets suit all facial sizes and come with ready-made eyeholes AND breathing holes – perfect for those sultry crusader campaigns. No more stuffy battles when you're wearing an Elkhorn!

Will improve your fighting. The top-of-the-range "Barbarossa" includes a vicious tusk, which is perfect for those in-your-face combat moments.

At Elkhorn we realize there's more to visors than mere fighting. They're a valuable social accessory – particularly at jousting tournaments. Have you noticed how the winning knight tilts his visor back in that devil-may-care way and comes forward to speak to his lady? How everybody loves it – especially when the visor clangs down and traps his tongue! All our visors have friction bearings, so you'll never get that with an Elkhorn!

Battle-tested at Jerusalem, Antioch, Acre, Poitiers, Crécy, Agincourt, and many, many more!!

NEW DEVELOPMENT FOR CRUSHED CITIZENS

LONDON BRIDGE – THE CAPITAL'S HOTTEST NEW ADDRESS!!

—1190—

The Mayor of London is **stunned** and **shocked** about new developments on his best bridge. The Mayor has recently spent three weeks in a darkened bedroom recovering from a stomach-stretching 320 eels, eaten during a royal banquet. When he finally opened his curtains and looked out over the River Thames he saw that **London Bridge was covered in houses.**

Plank

The thunderstruck official finally mustered the strength to make a comment. "I'd noticed some people lurking around with hammers and planks," he told the *Messenger*, "but I thought they were from Public Works come to mend the gallows or something. Imagine my astonishment when I realized what was going on."

Sick

It seems that city dwellers are sick and tired of having to squeeze into every nook and cranny in the overcrowded area within the city walls. Commuters too are weary of dreadful travel conditions, and have opted for direct action.

"The roads are awful," one London Bridge dweller told us. "They're always congested. And nothing's ever spent on maintenance. I almost drowned in a pothole last winter. So a bunch of us got together and thought, here's a bit of empty space right by where we work. Why not develop it and save ourselves all that travel?"

Arch

The 19-arch site, long a hazard for Thames boatmen, has proved remarkably popular. A church has already been built on it and prison authorities are planning a gatehouse where they can stick traitors' heads.

Redeveloped London Bridge, as seen from the prestigious Tower of London. The new properties are centrally located and convenient for river transportation.

GERMAN VICAR PANS GREEN MAN

—1190—

There I was, conducting a perfectly ordinary evensong. Suddenly I had this eerie feeling. I turned around and saw this little green man staring at me. I was so shocked I fainted!"

This report, from a **respectable German vicar**, is just one of thousands that are pouring in from all over Europe. What's happening? Are we being invaded by **beings** from another planet?

NO! The *Messenger* can reveal that it's nothing more than an elaborate plot by church architects. Asked to brighten up our churches and bring them into the 13th century, the jolly japesters filled them with **ancient pagan symbols**.

Trade

Green Men, as they're known in the design trade, are carvings of faces or figures covered in **leaves**. Once upon a time they represented gods of nature. **But not any more!** According to Hans Hocke of the Gothenburg Church Architects Association they now portray "benign images which represent renewal and resurrection".

Next

Next time you're in church have a good look around. You're bound to find a Green Man somewhere – and

A Green Man, lurking in the roof of a church.

probably just where you're least expecting him!

Let us know how you get on. These cheery fellows are tucked away in all kinds of odd corners. We'll give five groats for the most outrageous Green Man location in Europe.

FRENCH PLAY DIRTY!

The route to victory was through a castle toilet.

BAD KING JOHN'S TOP TEN TRIALS AND TORMENTS

—1216—

Was England's King John the worst monarch of the century? To celebrate the occasion of his death we've drawn up a chart of his toptastic ten biggest flops and disasters...

1. 1192 As a mere prince he **snatches** the English throne from brother King Richard who is off crusading. Beginning of era of extremely **high taxes**.

2. 1193 John made to look **utterly stupid** by hunky underworld dreamboat Robin Hood, who runs rings around him in Nottinghamshire.

3. 1194 Richard comes back from the crusades, and John has to give back the throne. (How demeaning!)

4. 1199 Inherits throne again and promptly starts losing all England's foreign territories. (Quite useless!)

5. 1214 His army is **defeated** by French at Battle of Bouvines, Flanders. Where is John at the time? Half a country away in Poitou "trying to organize a pincer movement". (So he says.)

6. 1214 Raises taxes an eye-watering 1,000 percent, making his nobles very irritated indeed. (Incredible folly.)

7. 1215 Forced by nobles to sign the **Magna Carta**, where he **gives away** enormous royal power and paves the way for democratic parliament. (Good for us, we admit. But for a king? ... Eternal embarrassment.)

8. 1215 French troops capture London. (**Will it never end?**)

9. 1216 Catches **dysentery**. (Typically low and incompetent.)

10. 1216 (again) **Dies.** Hurrah! But not before losing all his money, jewels, robes etc. in a marshy area of eastern England named the Wash. Known for ever after as "**the King who lost his clothes in the Wash**". (The final, wretched, unforgivable humiliation!)

Messenger comment: King John? – We say MORE LIKE KING CONTEMPTIBLE!!!

—1204—

Château Gaillard, England's strongest castle in France, **has fallen**. Built in 1190 by crusader hero King Richard the Lionheart, it includes the latest "tower and outer wall" castle-building technique, which Richard copied from his Muslim enemies.

"This castle is so well built," Rick used to boast, "that I could hold it if it was made of butter."

Weed

But Rick's successor, the ever-unpopular and weedy King John, has let it **slip through his fingers**. After a seven-month siege, during which the castle was constantly mined and bombarded with crossbow fire, French soldiers crept through a toilet on the outer wall and captured the whole castle.

"We were caught with our pants down," admits one English knight.

Chortle

"This is going to change the face of Europe," chortled French king Philip. "For years the English have been laying claim to territories that belong to our lot.

"From now on the English kings will have to content themselves with what they've got the other side of the Channel. After all, they can always have a go at invading Scotland."

Hanging

Military sources on both sides of the Channel agree that King John is a dolt. With Château Gaillard gone, the English kings have little hope of hanging on to territory in France, and that within a few decades they will have lost all their possessions in France.

England is on that island north of France, say the French, so the English ought to GET BACK THERE!

IT'S WAR! THREE YEARS LATE

Sun, sea and slaughter. English troops trounce the French fleet at Sluis, yesterday.

—1340—

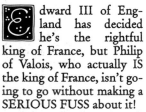

Edward III of England has decided he's the rightful king of France, but Philip of Valois, who actually IS the king of France, isn't going to go without making a SERIOUS FUSS about it!

Philip is also big pals with England's on-the-doorstep enemy Scotland, and Edward thinks Philip's about to invade England to help them! The result – France and England have officially opened the 100 Years War. **The trouble is it's taken three years to get started.**

"The original insults were exchanged as far back as 1337," admitted a French envoy. "But remember that 100 years of fighting takes some preparation. Both sides have had to **find** allies, **swap** additional insults, **raise** taxes, **train** armies, **invent** further insults and so on. **It's not a quick business.**"

Serious

Edward is taking the war so seriously he's issued a law commanding English peasants to stop playing football. Instead, they must polish up their skills with a bow and arrow. Anyone who disobeys faces public execution!

Rusty

Despite the long delay, hostilities started on a vigorous note with an unpleasant little campaign in the north of France when Edward's troops rampaged around for five weeks, burning villages and destroying crops. Things have livened up with a sea battle on Midsummer's Day, just outside the port of Sluis, in Flanders. The English fleet defeated their opponents thanks to superior longbow skills. Quick-firing archers, stationed on wooden "castles" at either end of their ships, made short work of the opposition. But the French vowed they would make a comeback.

"Just a minor hiccup," smiled King Philip of France. "Our troops were rusty after all that hanging around, that's all. You wait. **We're only in the first year and there's another 99 to come.**"

General

This doesn't seem to have affected the general populace. As far as anyone can tell, England and France are both getting ready for more. "Don't stop now," seems to be the general opinion. **The** *Messenger* **says, "Watch this space!"**

CRASH BANG WALLOP!
Calais comes a cropper

—1347—

After a siege lasting nearly a year, victorious English troops have been declared the owners of Calais. But angry citizens claim it was an unfair fight and are trying to have the decision overthrown. "We demand a re-siege!" stormed the Mayor of Calais. "The English cheated from start to finish. They have broken all the rules. **If this sort of thing continues it will ruin the good name of warfare.**"

Secret weapon

The French are hopping mad because the English have introduced a new weapon – gunpowder artillery.

"It's outrageous," said the Mayor. "We were expecting a standard siege, with ladders, heavy catapults, boiling oil, people starving slowly – you know, the usual kind of thing. But there was none of that. There I was, standing above the gate and having my midday laugh at the enemy, when there was this big bang and a cloud of smoke from the English lines.

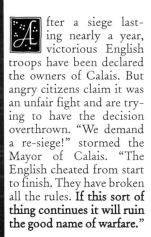

It looks like a vase, but it's far more dangerous.

"I thought a stove had blown up or something, but then I heard a whooshing noise and next thing I knew there was a filthy big metal arrow sticking halfway through the gate. It shook me up I can tell you! And that's not all. The English have got TEN of these things."

Stop fussing

When questioned about their new weapon, the English were unrepentant.

"It fires arrows, so basically it's no different from a longbow," said the Bombardier-General. "The only difference is that the arrows are **bigger and nastier**, they **travel farther and they do more damage.**"

He showed us one of these heavy iron weapons. As far as we could tell it looked harmless enough – unless you tried to pick it up!

"Appearances can be deceptive," he went on, tapping the cannon with his pointer. "It may look like a tipped-over vase. In fact it is a registered weapon of destruction. Now. Pay attention. What you do is fill the inside with gunpowder. Here! Then you stuff the arrow down the hole at the top. Here! Then you put a match to the hole at the other end. Here! And then you stand clear and cover your ears!"

Worse to come

When questioned by the *Messenger*, English diplomat Sir Castlemaine Faughecks responded, "We feel the enemy is complaining about nothing. In a short while everyone will have artillery pieces like these. And they will be firing increasingly sophisticated missiles – such as stone and metal balls."

MYSTERY PLAGUE ROCKS EUROPE

We've been bad says bishop

—1349—

As yet another city fell victim to the "Black Death", church leaders were in general agreement about the cause of the mystery plague. "We've all been very bad, and God is punishing us," the Bishop of Rheims told his congregation.

Although some sages blamed the plague on the movement of the planets, there were few who went along with this view at Rheims Cathedral.

Black blotches

Doctors have told patients to be on the lookout for the following symptoms – terrible aches and pains, fever, insanity, headaches, peevishness, and bursting blisters which ooze black blood. Physicians have been unable to come up with a sure-fire cure for the plague but ten-year-old treacle and chopped-up grass snake is currently the most popular remedy. "I can't recommend it highly enough," said Jean le Bonne, a baker from Brittany, shortly before he died.

Meanwhile looting of affected areas seems to be a continuing problem. Some cities and towns are completely deserted with their citizens either dying or fleeing into the countryside. "Looter looted my lute," said minstrel Jean de Chanson.

Doctors forecast the plague will last for three more years and kill a third of all Europeans.

Cemeteries reach bursting point. Authorities in some areas are digging emergency pits and trenches to deal with the situation while the plague deaths soar.

The plague. Bad news for man and beast.

Apprentices!

Do YOU want to make your way in the world? Join a guild. Once you've qualified in your chosen profession we offer you the chance to:

- get rich
- get richer
- attend riotous dinners
- wage trade wars
- wear fur hats and big gold chains

Don't delay! Hurry now to become a guild member. Remember, if you don't join a guild you'll never be able to put "Guild of Master Craftsmen" on your notepaper!

WHAT'S WAT GOT? NOT A LOT THAT'S WAT!

Wat Tyler gets the wrong side of the Mayor of London.

ROYAL EXCLUSIVE

Longbow is best says Edward III

Longbow — stone age? **Crossbow — too slow?**

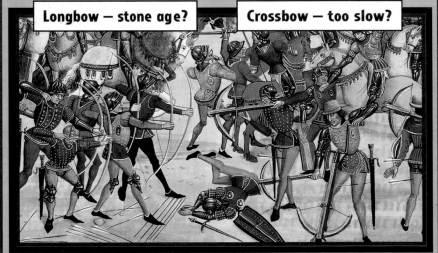

Technology special

— 1347 —

Top monarch Edward III added fresh fuel to the longbow versus crossbow debate yesterday when he claimed, "Longbows are best". Speaking to posh pals at Glastonbury Tournament, he said, "Anyone who says these new crossbows are better is talking out of their hat. Only last year we thrashed the French fair and square with longbows at the battle of Crécy."

Stone age

Arms experts rallied to his support. "Longbows have a quicker rate of fire, and all weather capability," said one leading knight.

But crossbow bosses were dismayed. Robert de Courcey of Crossbow Deathblow Inc. refused to concede. "Get out of the stone age. Crossbows are 100% more accurate and have a much higher hit-to-kill ratio."

— 1381 —

Londoners had the time of their lives when Wat Tyler and his "Peasants' Revolt" came to town. "Two days of sheer enjoyment," said one critic. "It's rip-roaring entertainment for all the family."

Revolting peasants

It all began when Wat, a tiler from Kent, organized a rebellion to complain about taxes. He marched with 10,000 peasants to London and proceeded to give the locals the show of the century.

"It was a magnificent spectacle," said Tom Titmuss, who lives in a fifth floor apartment on London Bridge. "They ransacked all the wealthy households. Ho ho ho! You should have seen John of Gaunt's face when they threw everything he owned into the Thames."

Heads on sticks

"Then they upped the tempo. If they saw anyone they thought might be a taxman they cut off his head and stuck it on a stick! Great stuff! After that they started burning all the government buildings and opening all the prisons. I tell you, honestly, it was one of the best rebellions I've seen in my life."

Surprise

The climax of the two-day event came when Wat and his men presented their demands to 14-year-old King Richard II.

"We were considerably surprised," said His Majesty. "But naturally we seized a pen and moved our hand back and forth over a piece of paper to suggest that we were re-writing the law as he wanted. As one does, you know."

But it was Wat who got the biggest surprise, when the Mayor of London came up and stabbed him to death.

The rebels were then so confused that they asked the King what to do next. He told them to go home and they did what he said.

Contrived

"If I had any complaint to make about the rebellion, it was the ending," said Tom Titmuss. "I thought it was contrived and, frankly, rather implausible. But then that's so often the problem with real-life dramas isn't it? So many strands, so many different parts, all those crowd scenes. I mean, something's got to give hasn't it?

"Still, I thought it was a jolly good effort. <u>Ten out of ten!</u>"

Richard II. Wat got his goat.

Bird break-through is bogus, says impatient patient

—1383—

Poorly patient Ron of Sallow, who doctors say is suffering from an imbalance of bodily humours, hit out yesterday at one of medicine's most recent and controversial techniques. Ron is disputing the accuracy of the so-called *Caladrius bird diagnosis* (C.B.D.) test.

In this procedure a Caladrius bird is placed in front of an ailing man to determine his chances of recovery. If the bird looks at him he will recover. If it looks away he will die.

"I just cawed to say I loathe you." Ron's bird turns him down.

Snuff

Ron's physician Jean de Tourniquet has refused him further treatment following a negative result, and patient Ron is getting more and more impatient! "I could tell at once that pesky bird didn't like me," fuming Ron told the *Messenger*.

Questioned about his health he went on, "It's my innards, they're not quite right. They ache a bit after I've eaten steamed pig fat and I get these blotches on my arms, but that doesn't mean I'm about to snuff it." Indeed, apart from a slight fever and an unpleasant rash Ron looked all right to us.

Rabbit

When we contacted Jean de Tourniquet he was quick to dismiss his patient's protests. "Ah, a tragic case," he told us, "and the C.B.D. test is never wrong. I've tried everything. A potion of rabbit droppings and mercury is an excellent remedy, but that doesn't seem to be working. I collected a couple of pints of blood from him, and that didn't work. Even a dose of wild lettuce and leeches hasn't cured him. Alas, we must wait for nature to take its course."

Right: Mercury and rabbit droppings cure fails after patient falls fowl of bird test.

GO GOTHIC WITH
TOP-NOTCH CONSTRUCTION

Is your attendance falling?

Don't blame your sermons. More than likely it's your cathedral that needs revising. Look around. Do you see: • Lurching spires? • Sagging pews? • Blocked transept? • Puddles in the belfry? Yes? Then call TOP-NOTCH CONSTRUCTION now! We have the answers to all your problems — and some you've never heard of.

Our architects are fully qualified masons who have spent years learning the secrets of their trade. Whether you want a custom-made nave, a vestry refit or a complete Gothic cathedral built from scratch, we'll supply you with accurate plans before you can say Evensong.

FLYING BUTTRESS
Build higher with this sure-fire support for sagging walls.

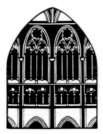

SPIRE
An absolute must! With one of these you're that little bit closer to heaven.

CLERESTORY
No, we don't know how to pronounce it either. But it lets in more light.

TOWER
Something to put a spire on. Or if a spire's that little bit too ostentatious, then something to put the bells in.

STAINED GLASS
The best in multichrome entertainment.

SAINTS
The congregation that never goes away. Good moral guidance for the rest of 'em too.

BELLS
Hear them chime. Carillons, peals, the lot. Also Dong, Dong, Dong, Dong.

TOMBS
Ultra-realistic pre-demise effigies of the departed. Legs crossed only if they've been on a crusade. Can also include dog under foot, wife by side, sword, packed-lunch etc.

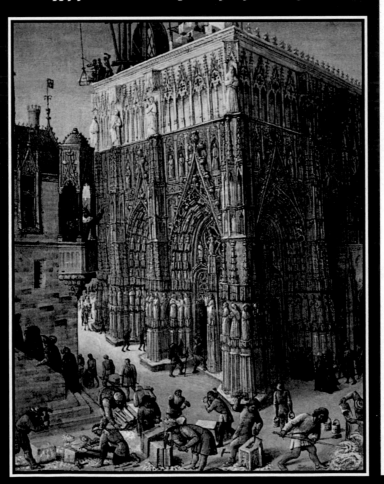

YOU AND YOUR STARS

with Patrick Thistle

The *Messenger's* own astrologer tells you what's in store...

Aquarius *January 21 to February 21*
There will be no plague, no famine, no war, your teeth will not fall out and if you're a servant you will be thrashed no more than five times a day. Really! What a wonderful year!

Pisces *February 21 to March 21*
All the portents suggest you will be taking a lot of baths this year. For heaven's sake don't. Apart from the obvious dangers to your health, people will start to avoid you. Only do this on doctor's orders.

Aries *March 21 to April 21*
This looks like a dreadful year for you. Your sheep will die, your cows will go mad, your swine will keel over and your fowl will perish. Honestly, it's a really bad one. If I were you I'd give this year a miss and go straight on to the next one.

Taurus *April 21 to May 21*
Those medicinal herbs you have been trying to grow for ages will start to pick up. Give the hyssop a lot of water in dry weather because it cures the colds which are going to afflict you in the winter. Did you cut back the marjoram hard last year? I hope so, because the new shoots are essential for the headaches which will plague you when you've recovered from the colds.

Gemini *May 21 to June 21*
Well, Geminis are meant to be well-balanced people. But there's one who isn't. Yes, I'm talking about you, Edward I of England. You are a violent and miserable type who should be more careful about who you subjugate. The Scots will never forgive you. And stop building all those castles to frighten the Welsh.

Cancer *June 21 to July 21*
Dig a big cellar and be prepared to hide there when Mongol hordes burn your house down. This precaution is a must for Cancerians who live in Hungary. The stars say that you will be ravaged, ransacked and ridiculed by a lot of rough types on horseback. So get digging now.

Leo *July 21 to August 21*
Bad news for Cathars. Your austere Christian faith has been popular in France and Italy for a few years, but the established church doesn't like the way you're making it look corrupt and worldly. Expect an extremely violent reaction in the next few years (especially if you're reading this between 1200 and 1240).

Virgo *August 21 to September 21*
You will make your usual pilgrimage to Compostela in Spain, you will eat your usual vast quantities of oysters when you get there, and this time, for once, YOU WILL NOT EAT A BAD ONE! Hurrah!

Libra *September 21 to October 21*
Librans are harmonious, charming people who like to decorate their homes in pastel shades of brown. What a shame, then, that this year is going to be one of rich, exotic hues with gaudy clothes being imported from the East and garish stained-glass windows popping up everywhere. I advise you to stay indoors until the Gothic era has ended. Stock up with plenty of turnips!

Scorpio *October 21 to November 21*
A rare configuration of stars suggests that Frederick Barbarossa, the Holy Roman Emperor, will drown one of you slowly in a wine barrel to see if he can detect any sign of your soul escaping. Condemned criminals should be especially cautious.

Sagittarius *November 21 to December 21*
You will perform many feats of heroism with your trusty bow. But whatever you do, don't let it get too damp. This has led to many a poor performance in major battles.

Capricorn *December 21 to January 21*
There is some uncertainty here. The planets are entering a particularly auspicious phase for Capricornians. They show every likelihood of prosperity and good fortune, particularly if your birthday is on the eighth. On the other hand, my birthday is on the eighth, and I'm having a rotten time. Astrology?

Messenger COMMENT

WE'VE NEVER HAD IT SO GOOD!

Remember how it used to be before we got medieval? Dark Ages, famine, backward farming practices, few towns and merchants, squabblesome populace, always being invaded by people in horned helmets. For goodness sake, **it was so bad we thought the world was going to end! (And what a joke that was, eh?)**

Now look at us! If we're not sitting pretty then I don't know what we're doing. More opportunities are open to us than ever before. We can:

Go on crusades	*Live in bigger towns*
Catch plague	*Catch more plague*
Build vast stone castles	*Wear fancy clothes*
Persecute religious minorities	*Put spices in our food*
Make pilgrimages	*Attend tournaments*

We couldn't do that in the Dark Ages, could we? **No Sir!** So what does this say for us? It says we're a go-ahead era, that's what! And if anybody wants to make jokes about "being Middle-Aged" **they'd better be wearing protection.**

What next?

We took to the streets to ask our readers what they think the future holds. There was one thing you all agreed on: the next Age is going to be called the **Renaissance.** Otherwise, your answers showed the intelligent variety we'd expect from *Messenger* readers. Here's a few of them:

"Plague! Lots more plague!"

"Bigger cities. Swankier palaces. Funnier clothes."

"Perspective. I foresee a far greater use of perspective in art. That, and a growth in interior design. Chapel ceilings will be particularly magnificent."

"Wars! Many more wars!"

"Seats of learning will be everywhere. Much more comfortable than these old stools."

"The use of telescopes to show that the earth orbits the sun."

"I think it will be the age of the potato, if they ever discover the country it grows in."

"Handwriting will be finished! So will parchment! It'll be printing and cheap, easy-to-read books made out of paper."

"There'll be more attempts to find a sea route to China. Who knows – they might even discover America if they go the wrong way."

"The end of the world will come in AD1500."

"No it won't."

Too many fast days equals a lot of baggy habits for Europe's monks.

FOOD IN THE FAST LANE

onks are too thin! That's what leading abbots are saying as they introduce sweeping changes to monastery menus. There are more than 200 foodless fast days (when monks don't eat for the good of their souls) on the Christian calendar – including Fridays and Lent. Hungry monks found they were only eating for a total of 23 weeks every year. The result? **A lot of baggy habits.**

Fast

Now new regulations say monks can eat anything they like on a fast day **so long as it's not meat.** If that sounds boring, then think again. The ingenious cowlheads have come up with some mouth-watering recipes to tempt even the most jaded palate.

Tuck

Anything that lives in water has been classified as a FISH, so monks can tuck into such delicious dishes as fried frog with steamed turnip, and boiled beaver with hot buttered swede.

But some church chiefs are warning that relaxing the rules regarding clerical catering will lead to a waistline explosion, and **emaciated monks** will become **fat friars** before you can say **"A whole roast ox please, WITH ALL THE TRIMMINGS!"**

ARE YOU EATING A BALANCED DIET?

Frumpy and dumpy after all those Christmas parties?

Get back into shape with the *Messenger* diet.

Our expert nutritionists have drawn up an easy-to-follow menu to suit all pockets. This shows just what you should be eating at each meal.

PEASANT	NOBLE
Rye bread *Sliver of cheese*	Eggs *White bread* *Milk*
BREAKFAST	
Rye bread *Sliver of cheese*	Pastries *Bit of cheese* *Spicy eels* *Fish cakes* *Sturgeon* *"The best roast that may be had."* *Oysters* *Venison* *Blancmange*
LUNCH	
Rye bread *Sliver of cheese* *Cabbage** *(Sundays only)*	As for lunch *but add nibbles,* *apéritifs, hogsheads* *of wine and kegs* *of beer...*
SUPPER	

*Omit if this causes wind and discomfort after meals. These are common symptoms of starvation and cabbage will make them worse.

Property for sale

BIG CASTLE. Not yet stormed. Ramparts need some attention but otherwise OK. Three large living rooms and banqueting hall. Turret toilets empty onto peasants below. Delightful outlook. **Box 443.**

TOWN LOT. Derelict house and garden. Plague repossession. Looks fine from outside. Heaven knows what lies within. **Box 324.**

KRACK. Funny name, fantastic castle. Beautifully situated in Holy Land, with arrowslits, double walls, interior citadel and all-around protection. Built by crusaders but currently occupied by Muslim troops. Available to anyone with enough troops. **Box 657.**

HOLE. Well-placed hole set in dry bank on outskirts of pleasant village. Ditch within easy reach for washing, etc. Any reasonable offer. **Box 846.**

Lady Penelope's
Q&A

HUNGRY FOR ADVICE?
HERE'S FOOD FOR THOUGHT

HOLES

 I am told that I should supply trenchers at every meal. Why? I don't want people digging holes in the floor.

Don't be silly. Trenchers are what you put your guests' food on. They're thick slices of bread. And when they get too soggy you just throw them under the table for the dogs.

RUBBISH

 Our castle needs a new midden. Where can I get one?

As everyone knows, a midden is just another word for a scrapheap. You can buy them ready made but the best way is to start your own. Simply choose a place downwind and put your kitchen scraps there. In a few months it'll be a perfectly acceptable pile of rotten food. Some people say you should move your midden at regular intervals to stop it from getting smelly. But I've found that my peasants will do the job for me. If I let them scrabble through it at regular intervals everything turns out smell-free and satisfactory.

SMOKE

 Dear Lady P. Our manor has a big hall. It's very nice and we eat there every day. But I've noticed that we spend mealtimes coughing and retching. Afterwards we smell strongly of smoke. What can I do?

Well, it sounds to me as if your hall is one of the old-fashioned types with a fireplace in the middle. What you need is one of the new hearths which fits into the wall and has a decent chimney to get rid of all that smoke. That'll deal with the coughing and the nasty smell. As for the retching, are you by any chance eating mud and grass? If so, stop it at once. The Dark Ages are over, you know!

CHEESY

 As a simple villein I live off rye bread and cheese. But sometimes I can't find cheese in the shops. Any answer to my dilemma?

 There's a delightful dish called "False cheese on rye bread". What you do is take your usual slice of bread, put it on the table, and then pretend you have a piece of cheese to go with it. It brings out the rye taste to perfection. It has a quick preparation time and is very economical too!

PRONGS

 I've got this wonderful idea. When we sit down to dinner everyone just shovels it in with a spoon and a piece of bread. How unseemly! Why not have a metal implement with several prongs in order to carry morsels cleanly to your mouth?

You're talking of something called a fork. They exist elsewhere but I'm afraid they haven't caught on in Europe. We're not that advanced. Besides, what would it do for a fellow's fighting reputation if he was caught using a sissy thing like that? Forget it, that's my advice.

FARMING NEWS

IT'S GOODBYE TO RIDGE-AND-FURROW!

S trip farming is to be axed as the landed gentry push through laws to change the face of farming.

For centuries peasants have farmed little strips of land about two paces wide. Nobody knows why. But this is how it's always been done. As a result, farms have become a higgledy-piggledy mess of ridges and furrows. The latest legislation intends to replace ridge-and-furrow with new units called **"fields"**.

Delight

"The field is a delightfully simple concept," says one landowner. "What you do is clear the peasants off. Then till the place up, and plant hedges to divide the area into organized plots which will make **me** more **money**."

Not everyone is happy with this new concept. "Our traditional country way of life is disappearing," moaned peasant Cedric Sodd, whose family has worked the same strip for ten generations. "I blame all you city folk, with your meddling and your weekend homes. I bet you people think strip farming's an adult game for landowners. How stupid can you get."

Headache

Other peasants are more optimistic. "Strip farming has been nothing but a

One of those new-style FIELDS – at the cutting edge of agricultural technology.

headache," says Humbert of Oxley. "We lie awake at night wondering whether we're tilling our own strip or someone else's. It's difficult remembering which one is yours. Nobody knows for sure. Life will be much easier and neater when we have a little square patch with a hedge around it."

Rhomboid

"You needn't stop with squares, either," enthused

his friend Dogbert "You could have rectangles, rhomboids, parallelograms, triangles – anything, in fact! It would give the landscape a lovely patchwork effect. Visually, the present system is incredibly monotonous. It's like looking at a vast pair of corduroy trousers."

And in the future people will stop and say. "Look at those little fields. How quaint! This is what we'd always imagined the countryside to be like!"

WHEY-HEY! WHAT'S ALL THIS THEN?

W hen it comes to whey, Europe is the world's TOP producer. In fact, farmers are producing so much of the stuff that they can hardly even give it away.

Lumps

"Well," said one farmer, "when you think about it, it's not surprising we can't get rid of it. Whey's the watery mixture with lumps in it that is what's left over when you've finished making cheese. It's quite revolting. Who'd want to eat that?"

Fussy

Lady Muffet, a long-standing member of the Whey Marketing Board,

disagrees. "People are too fussy about their diets. In my day, everybody ate whey – if you were lucky you had some curds in it too. You could sit down on any old tuffet and just tuck in. But things were different then. I remember the country was full of spiders. Gosh they were a menace. They appeared from nowhere, wiggling their little legs and trying to sit down beside you. Some girls were frightened away. Me, I trod on them. They soon got the message."

Minority

Muffet is in the minority. With or without spiders, no one wants to eat whey nowadays.

Whey. Here's where it all begins...

FARMING NEWS

PLANET OF THE SHEEP – "It's like a baa-d dream"

While shepherds amuse themselves, sheep plot to TAKE OVER THE WORLD.

Bleating sweeps Europe

The human race is no longer in control. With **eight million** sheep roaming England alone – that's three sheep to every human – scared farmers are wondering if they've started something they can't stop.

It began low-key, with a few farmers moving their flocks around the country in search of better grazing. The result was so good that everybody got on the bandwagon. And now? **Gigantic flocks of sheep are moving up and down Europe eating everything in sight.**

Frantic

"There's nothing we can do," claimed a frantic shepherd. "Economically, there's no way we can compete against sheep. We don't grow wool and you can't make us into bagpipes, candles or parchment. What chance do we have? This is the end of human supremacy. In the very near future this planet will be run by sheep."

Bulky

We asked our agricultural specialist for his opinion, and he told us: "When you look at it, the sheep is far too bulky to become top dog. In an expanding-population scenario they would soon cover the landscape completely. Then they would die because there was no grass to eat.

"My own feeling is that if there **is** any threat to humanity it will come from **rabbits.** They're small, unobtrusive and live underground. **By the time they're ready to take over we'll be totally unprepared.**"

OUCH! PIGS GET IT IN THE EAR

Runaway pigs – another hazard for city dwellers.

When little Prince Louis was riding through Paris the last thing he expected was to be knocked off his horse by a runaway pig. But that's what happened last month, leaving His Royal Highness with a fractured skull, and bacon as No.1 on the butcher's hit list. "That pig is sausages!" yelled Prince Lou from his sickbed.

The anguished royal has put a price on the head of every porker in town. And he's hired the public executioner to do the dirty work.

"It's a lot different from what I'm used to," admits "Max-the-Axe" de Slamm, whose nimble beheading technique has earned him the Chamois D'Or three years running. "Normally it's just a fellow on a block and you whack his head off. These pigs aren't half as easy. First you've got to catch them – and they're slippery little beggars I can tell you."

Necks

With Mad Max on the lookout, Parisian farmers are worried for their future. "Contrary to popular belief, the town is quite a rural place," said one spokesman. "Almost everybody keeps some sort of livestock. Cows, sheep, chickens, pigs – you name it. Normally they're well behaved and nobody cares. Then you get one incident like this and everyone's breathing down our necks."

Capital cattle

Farmers have started moving their pigs around town to avoid capture. But Max is on top of things.

"I can hear 'em! Grunting and snorting! I wait around the corner of an alley. If there's the slightest snuffle I'm out there with my axe and **WHAM!** One curly-tail less!"

So far Max has caught two elderly pigs and three people with bad colds. WAY TO GO, MAX!

WHAT'S NEW AT THE SPANISH INQUISITION?

We meet the man in the know

It's a ghastly business. Inquisitor-General Señor X shows some heretics what happens if you step out of line.

"Heretics galore!" smiled Señor X, the Inquisitor-General. "It's been absolutely frantic out there. We've got more than we can deal with! Already we're sending out for extra firewood. And our inquisitors are worked to the bone. So if any of your readers know how to crank a rack we'd be delighted to hear from them."

Señor X – being publicity shy, he refuses to reveal his real name – has been at the cutting edge of the Inquisition for years. His job – to seek out heretics, the greatest threat to a stable ordered society since the Black Death.

Slippers

But when *Messenger* reporter Rosie de Jonqueville visited him at his home in Seville, he was wearing slippers and a casual tunic and was in an expansive mood.

So, we asked, exactly who is the Inquisition interested in interviewing?

"It's all to do with church regulations," he said, fiddling absent-mindedly with a thumbscrew. "If believers show the slightest sign of disagreeing with the sacred principles of the Catholic faith, that's heresy, and we inquist them. This means we ask them a lot of searching questions about their faith. Granted, they're not easy questions. But we have some very simple physical tests for those who find the questions too complex. The point of it all is to get the accused to change his mind – or recant, as we inquisitors call it."

Pain

And what are those tests?

"Ho ho!" winked Señor X. "I think that would be telling, wouldn't it?"

Do those tests involve physical pain?

"Well, yes. I think that would be a fair assumption. But only for the best possible reasons, of course."

Pain such as being beaten on the feet? Burned at the stake?

"Well, perhaps now and then, and only as a last resort. You've obviously been listening to too many sensationalist town criers, young lady."

So what makes a heretic, we asked.

"Oh, anything. It doesn't really matter. Any slight deviation will do."

Foreign

Like being foreign?

"Absolutely! That's prime evidence. We devote a lot of our time to people who look different. After all, if you're from somewhere else there's no telling what nasty religious habits you might have picked up. And talking about habits, we've had endless trouble with the friars. These Dominicans and Franciscans! Always having to do things their own way. Really! They shouldn't question the authority of the church. They bring it on their own heads."

Harmless

Señor X looks perfectly harmless. **But while his tunic is stained with egg and gravy, his reputation is stained with blood.**

Does this worry him?

"Oh no," he replied firmly. "Our aim is to enforce religious unity throughout Europe. There's only one faith – the Catholic faith – and **it's my job to make sure it stays that way**. If that means we have to torture people, and burn a couple of thousand at the stake, then **so be it**. It's worth all the trouble!"

HOW SUPERSTITIOUS ARE YOU?

__Prof. "Omen" Tally de Raynjd gets to grips with what makes the world go around.__

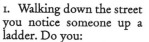

Life's a mystery isn't it? Things just happen out of the blue. Plague. Warfare. Famine. Dental decay. You name it. And we haven't the first idea what caused them.

But what do YOU think? I've drawn up a simple test so that you can tell whether you're one of the new-fangled scientific types or a straightforward believer in good old superstition.

Give it a go and see how YOU rate. It could change your life!

1. Walking down the street you notice someone up a ladder. Do you:
a) Walk under the ladder.
b) Walk around the ladder.
c) Kick the ladder down?

2. At a party you meet a man who introduces himself as a wizard. Do you:
a) Roll your eyes.
b) Put out two fingers in the sign of the evil eye.
c) Put out two fingers and poke him in the eyes?

3. You find you've got an unlucky 13 people sitting down to dinner. Do you:
a) Serve the spiced goat before it gets cold.
b) Find another guest.
c) Kill one of them?

4. A black cat crosses your path. Do you:
a) Think "That'll be Tibbins from next door."
b) Think "Oh! I'm going to have some good luck."
c) Strap the cat to the front of your shoe so you always have good luck?

5. An old woman comes up and says, "I can cure that wart on your nose." Do you:
a) Say "Thank you."
b) Tell the church authorities.
c) Burn her at the stake?

6. Accidentally you break a mirror. Do you:
a) Swear under your breath.
b) Look forward to seven years' bad luck.
c) Pretend someone else did it and tell them that if they don't take the blame they'll have seven years' bad luck starting right here and now?

7. You come across a wishing well. Do you:
a) Have a drink.
b) Throw in a coin and make a wish.
c) Storm the well, declare it your own, then take out all the money except for one small penny which you attach to a string and drop in and out to make multiple wishes?

8. You see a bright light streaking across the night sky. Do you:
a) Say, "Ah! It's a comet!"
b) Confess all your sins because the end is nigh.
c) Go on a drunken orgy of arson and looting because the end is nigh?

9. A calf is born with two heads. Do you:
a) Go, "Iiiimm. Weird calf."
b) Predict certain calamity for your village.
c) Burn down the village to spare it from certain calamity?

SO HOW DID YOU DO?

If you scored mostly 'a's you are not at all superstitious. This means you are a scientifically-minded person and completely out of touch with society. You are missing out on a lot of exciting hopes and fears. I bet people think you're pretty odd. Actually, I'm surprised you haven't been dunked in the nearest pond to see if you're a witch.

If you scored mostly 'b's then you respect all the current superstitions and are a normal, honest-to-goodness, law-abiding citizen.

If you scored mostly 'c's then you are not only superstitious but brutal, loutish, bad tempered, violent, destructive and an out-and-out swine. __Congratulations! You're a perfect medieval specimen. Have you thought of going for high office?__

DON'T KILL THAT SPIDER!

A superstition is born

We like to think of superstitions as ancient things. Not a bit of it! Robert the Bruce, king of Scotland, made a brand new one only the other day.

Down

"I'd had a run of bad luck," he said. "I'd lost two battles to the English. They even executed three of my brothers. I was down and out. Things were so bad I was even living in a cave. And I had to think up a new tactic. I was desperate!

"Then I noticed a spider crawling up the cave wall. It fell off once... twice... but on the third attempt it got there. So I thought, if a spider can do that, so can I!"

Thrashing

"So I rushed out and gave the English the biggest thrashing of their lives at a place called Bannockburn. They won't forget that in a hurry. They thought they owned Scotland. Now it looks like they're going to have to recognize we're an independent country. Pah! What a shower !"

Brave Bruce's victory has given us not one but TWO superstitions. "Don't kill a spider!" and "Third time lucky!"

Ticking

It's people like this keep the world ticking over. Hooray for Bruce, says the *Messenger*. Let's have a lot more like him!

Bannockburn – third time lucky for brave Bruce!

"MY QUARTERED ESCUTCHEON IS PURFLED AND HURTY!"

And whose wouldn't be?

Knowing the man behind the visor is so much easier with new style heraldry.

Relax. It's not some nasty medical condition. In normal language this means, "My shield has a gold rim and is divided into four sections with a pattern of blue dots."

What?

Don't laugh. It's all part of the latest craze sweeping every court in Europe – <u>heraldry</u>.

Who's who

It all started with the crusaders. Unable to tell who anyone was once he'd pulled down his visor, they came up with the idea of giving themselves individual emblems and painting them on their shields.

"It worked very well," said Raymond of Toulouse. "Before, we were just anonymous lumps of metal on horses. With the new system you could look at a knight's shield and say 'Ah! Three Rabbits Rampant! That'll be Fritz of Thuringia!'"

Stag Trippant

"Eventually, things got a bit out of hand. With more and more crusaders arriving in the Holy Land people started inventing all kinds of loopy emblems. You'd get things like a Stag Trippant (a prancing stag), or a Savage Affronté (a naked wildman with a beard).

And then the enemy thought it was a good idea and started copying us. Frankly, it got very confusing, particularly in the bigger battles. But at least it brightened the place up."

Fretty Golpes

Now everyone's jumped on the bandwagon. A coat-of-arms is a must-have for every self-respecting knight, crusader or not. You can't get into a tournament without one.

And to make it extra exclusive they've invented this weird language that's half French and half English to go with it. Fretty Golpes? That's eight purple balls. Wolf Salient? A leaping wolf. Fessways Escarbuncles? A row of jewels. Lucy Gules? A red fish.

Terribly simple

We asked the man in charge of English heraldry why it had to be so complicated.

"No, no. It's not at all complicated," enthused Sable Basilisk. "Nor is it exclusive. Why, I bet there's a coat-of-arms for your paper. Let's look it up. Ah! Here we are. Messenger: a Pegasus, Current (ducally gorged and chained). There. What could be simpler?"

What indeed?

Health Extra

"I'M NOT DEAD!" INSISTS CORPSE

"Oh yes you are," says priest

Chantalle Lemon, a lace-maker from Flanders, was hopping mad when she learned yesterday that she was officially "dead".

The 23-year-old Assistant Darning Executive told us her story.

"I'd gone home to get a new darning mushroom when I suddenly fell asleep. After a little while I was awoken by a blanket being thrown over me. I stayed absolutely still because I thought it was a burglar, and I didn't want to disturb him in case he was violent. Then I felt myself being loaded onto a stretcher and carried out of the house.

"I was taken to a place which was obviously a church. It smelled all musty, and there were people chanting in Latin. I stayed still out of respect until I realized they were reading prayers for the dead over me. At that I threw off the blanket and said, 'Here! What's going on?'

Castanets

"Imagine my astonishment when the priest gave me a pair of castanets.

"'What's this for?' I asked. 'Flamenco lessons?'

"'No,' he said. 'You've got leprosy. You're now officially dead and we're going to take you to a leper colony where you can live with other official corpses. Whenever you come near us ordinary people you must rattle your castanets. Oh yes. And here's a pair of gloves because we don't want you touching us.'

Not a spot

"Apparently someone had spotted a white spot on my hand, which is one of the first signs of leprosy. I pointed out that it was just a bit of lace fluff which had been caught between my

Chantalle, yesterday.

fingers but they took absolutely no notice.

"'Sic mortuus mundo, vivens iterum Deo,' said the priest. Roughly translated this means: God thinks you're alive but we don't. Then he took me away to the leper colony. And that was that."

Medical review

Chantalle is pressing for a review but nobody will come near her in case they catch the dreaded disease.

"Sadly there is no cure for leprosy and none of us wants to risk it," said a medical spokesman.

MISTRESS MANNERS

The lady in the know offers her advice on all matters of etiquette

No blunder too bad! No faux pas too frightful! No gaffe too ghastly! Mistress Manners delves deep into her social treasure-chest and produces a gem to meet your every requirement.

Mistress Manners shares her headwear wisdom

Humble

Dear Mistress Manners,
I am a humble lad who works in my lord's kitchen. I perform all my duties with great care and humility. There is one problem, however. Come dinner I have to turn the spit above the central fireplace in the banqueting hall. This is a long, hot business. In fact it gets so hot that I long to throw off all my clothes and perform my chore stark naked. **Would this be acceptable in polite society?**
Andy Ladd, The Henhouse, Castle Keep, Northants.

Dear Master Ladd,
By all means. It is quite common to enter the finest banqueting hall and find the spit turner wearing nothing but his birthday suit. But when roasting some of the fattier animals, such as pig, you might like to wear an apron so that you don't get a sizzling great gob of lard just where you don't want it. OK?

Deep shame

Dear Mistress Manners,
I am deeply ashamed. I went last week to a public bathhouse. To my horror I emerged clean and fresh as a daisy. Now everybody shuns me because I do not smell like them, i.e. like an old midden. **What can I do to rectify this appalling gaffe?**
Name and address withheld by request.

Dear Peter Parsnip of 74 Castle Lane, Warwick,
You have been very improper indeed. As everybody knows, bath-houses are sinks of vice and iniquity, and while it is quite proper to indulge in vice and iniquity it is not done to flaunt the fact by being clean. What you must do is find the smelliest dungheap in town and roll in it. This will restore your normal, socially acceptable stink. In the future, avoid bathhouses at all costs. If you want to wash, may I recommend a thorough scouring with a mixture of mutton fat and wood ash. This is used by the majority of households and will allow you to smell like everyone else.

Wretched retch

Dear Mistress Manners,
I work and live in the basement of a very old and important castle. Normally my duties do not take me upstairs. But the other day I had some time on my hands and hearing that the castle was being attacked, I took the opportunity to make my first visit to the ramparts. It was very exciting strolling past all these busy bowmen, and nobody took any notice of me at all. But when I looked over the edge I was so overcome by vertigo that I lost my lunch all over the foreign gentlemen who were attacking us from below. Imagine my shame! **Can you tell me if there is an international sign of apology which I can make should such a dreadful thing happen again?**
Ron Cudlipp, Ye Olde Importante Castle, Hole.

Dear Ron,
The answer to your question is Yes. First stick out your tongue to get the gentlemen's attention. Then place your thumb against your nose and rapidly fan your fingers to and fro. This indicates that your actions were involuntary. They, in turn, will shake their fists to show that they understand. They may make certain other gestures involving one or sometimes two fingers, and perhaps also the forearm. But it is unnecessary to go into such social intricacies. The important thing, after these initial overtures, is to give them a small gift to say you are sorry. Oil is traditionally used. Don't bother with fancy bottles or wrapping paper. Simply boil it up in a cauldron and tip it over the edge. I guarantee that they will be visibly moved by your apology.

Half-gnawed

Dear Mistress Manners,
A query about dinner etiquette. When I'm eating I belch, I wipe my greasy fingers on my clothes, I throw half-gnawed bones over my shoulder, I pick my nose and suck my teeth noisily to get rid of all the leftovers stuck in them. For some reason nobody will speak to me. **Am I doing anything wrong?**
Ivo de Cologne, Chateau Sauvage, Savoy.

Dear Ivo,
Your demeanour at dinner is quite normal. Possibly your problem has financial roots. I'm sure that if you appeared at table with a large bag of coins and flung them around shouting, "There's plenty more where that came from," everyone would want to know you.

NEXT WEEK – COURTING SPECIAL

JUDGE SLAMS ROGUE PUBLISHER

MONK'S MONEY-MAKING MONASTERY SHAME

Thomas Minky, 36, ex-monk and self-confessed fraudster, hung his head in shame as Judge Roger de Floggem sentenced him to a life of silence in a Cistercian monastery.

"And think yourself lucky the Inquisition didn't get to you first," thundered the Judge as Minky was led from court.

Beasts

It all began with the new vogue for illuminated bestiaries. Marketed by monks as "pocket zoos", these hugely popular books show pictures of all known animals and are widely read throughout the continent. Money-minded Minky, who has been thrown out of several monasteries, decided to give them a new edge. Setting himself up as an independent publisher he used his illustrating skills to produce bestiaries like no other.

On-the-edge

"Usually we concentrate on rabbits, sheep, fish and the usual kiddie stuff," said one leading abbot. "But Minky took it to its limits. He played up the phoenixes, unicorns and all kinds of on-the-edge creatures. People bought his books like hot cakes. They thought it was fun."

But fun turned to fraud when Minky started to advertise these creatures locally, offering them as pets.

"They couldn't believe their luck," explained the abbot. "Minky would say, 'Young unicorns ready. Horns starting to grow', and he'd be flooded with cash. Of course, when the unicorn came it was just a foal with a lump on its head which got better in a week. The phoenix was nothing more than a singed chicken."

Rumbled

Minky's money-maker was rumbled when wildfowl breeder Jack "The Hen" McVitie sent off for some Barnacle Geese, which Minky claimed could be grown from a bush which sprouted from a barnacle. But when McVitie's barnacle failed to sprout he called trading officers who launched a full investigation into Minky's activities.

Eminent

"I've seen a fair few geese and ducks in my time," said one officer, "and in my considered and very eminent opinion Barnacle Geese come from *eggs* not barnacles."

Unfortunately, Minky had already sold over 200 barnacles to gullible customers, and when the news broke an angry crowd gathered outside his offices.

The authorities were forced to take him into protective custody.

Serves him right

Following a three-hour trial, Judge Floggem passed sentence. "Thomas Minky, your publishing house is a disgrace. You have misled the public. You have sold them Talking Hedge-hogs and Fortune-telling Rabbits. You have even sold them Burn-and-Come-Again Phoenixes. In the case of the Barnacle Goose you have been particularly deceitful. You have brought disappointment to thousands of dissatisfied customers and are a menace to society. If I ever see you again you will be sent to the gallows and hung by the neck until you are dead."

Above – Minky is apprehended by a trading officer. Below – the infamous advert.

Parchment or paper – which is best?

Peter Pier, a respected dealer in antiquarian manuscripts, was horrified when he found he had been sold a dud. For years Pier had scoured local markets in search of an illustrated manuscript of *Europe's Fighting Men*. When he found one he was delighted. But when he got it home he was less than happy.

"Would you believe it," he fumed. "What I thought was a perfectly good piece of **parchment** turned out to be nothing less than **paper**! It's outrageous! I warn all readers to be on the lookout."

Substances

The problem is that paper and parchment are both whitish substances on which you can write. To most people they look identical. But parchment is much sturdier and will last several lifetimes. Paper, on the other hand, is skimpy stuff which falls to pieces after a few years. So how do you pick the genuine article? We discussed the problem with parchment industry spokesman Maurice de Mouton.

Mashed and rolled

Mouton told us that paper was made of bits of cloth, which had been shredded, soaked, mashed and rolled. Parchment on the other hand was made of lamb's hide, finely scraped to a smooth finish. "Paper looks like parchment," he told us, "but it tears easily. It's **cheap**, it's **nasty**, and the only thing it's good for is **printing on**. However, we'll have to wait until the middle of the 15th century for that. I'd say there's no possible reason to use paper instead of parchment, unless you're a peasant who can only afford the cheapest materials. And if you are, what are you doing writing anyway – **you're supposed to be illiterate.**"

TEMPUS FUGIT "TIME FLIES"

Yes It Does when you join the Troubadour Express. Here at TE we're in tune with the century. We're a book club with a difference – because we realize that most of you can't read. What we offer is the chance to become a literary lion without even having to turn a page. Choose any single cult classic from the list of titles below, and one of our select team of troubadours will visit your home to read or sing it to you. If you're not completely satisfied, just send him back to us and we will refund your money.

KING ARTHUR

The tale of a plucky king whose Knights of the Round Table fight ceaselessly to defend England against foreign invaders. Taken from an original tale of a plucky Welsh king whose knights fight ceaselessly to defend their land against English invaders. Love, betrayal, heroism and magic. This one has it all. The most popular saga of the century.

ROMAN DE LA ROSE

Courtly love at its best. Who can resist this account of chivalric knights pining for their unattainable ladies? Cupid fires his bow and the impetuous heroes try to find the arrow. Do they succeed? Wait and see!

CANTERBURY TALES

A group of pilgrims are on their way to Canterbury. Where do they come from? What stories can they tell? Geoffrey Chaucer works his usual magic in this intimate peek into everyday English life. (You'll love the Wife of Bath's tale!)

DIVINE COMEDY

Wordsmith Dante Alighieri breaks new ground here. No laughs but plenty of excitement as he leads you on a voyage of self-exploration through hell, purgatory and paradise. Features beautiful heroine Beatrice – familiar to anyone who knows Dante's other works – plus the Italian superhero and author Virgil.

Not to be missed under any circumstances.

PIERS PLOWMAN

A moral tale for the moral-minded. Piers, a hard-working peasant who eats brown bread and horse beans, is disgusted at the farm hands who spend their time drinking ale and singing "Hey Trolli-Lolli." See them get their comeuppance! A must for anyone interested in contemporary ethics.

MAGNA CARTA

A fascinating snippet from the archives. This historic document gives the full 63 clauses which enabled English barons to break free from tyrant King John. Listen to the rolling declarations:

"No free man shall be taken or imprisoned, or stripped of his rights or possessions, or outlawed or exiled, or in any way ruined..." Stirring stuff! Our storytellers read the names of the barons who signed it with particular vim.

DECAMERON

Giovanni Boccaccio has excelled himself here. The Black Death is raging in Florence and a group of citizens have run for the hills. The result? One hundred of the very best short stories to be found anywhere. Will have you on the edge of your seat.

THE BIBLE

Settle down to a few Psalms with the world's best-selling book.

NOW YOU SEE IT NOW YOU DON'T!

MIRACLE EYESIGHT INVENTION GETS THUMBS-DOWN

Roger "Egghead" Bacon has come up with yet another wacky gadget. The loopy English inventor shook financial institutions with his last suggestion: an enormous mirror which enemy countries could use to spy on each other. **Now he has gone one step further with a device to cure the partially sighted.**

V-shaped

"I haven't fine-tuned it yet," admitted raving Roger. "But the basic principle is you get two pieces of see-through stuff – glass would do excellently – then you cut them into convex shapes (that's bulging outwards from the sides to the middle, for the non-scientists among us), and hold them in front of your eyes. If you wanted to be really sophisticated you could join them with a V-shaped strip of metal and hang them on your nose. Just how they'd stay there, if you wanted to use them for reading, I don't know. But that's a minor wrinkle which can be ironed out at production stage."

Mixed reception

Financial experts responded coolly to news of Roger's invention.

"I don't envisage volume sales," said one medical

SPEC-TACULAR!!

An eminent scholar models Bacon's latest invention. But will the glass and metal "spectacles" catch on?

analyst from the Hello & Welcome Foundation. "I can see there might be a market for this in monasteries where they have to spend a lot of time peering at little words in dark rooms. But most people spend their time looking at big things – castles, towers, monasteries, endless vistas of ridge-and-furrow farmland and enormously fat lords, to give just a few examples. For the majority such a device would be completely useless."

However, Roger has strong support from the Royal Institute of Alchemists.

The President gave his wholehearted backing to Bacon's new idea.

Water to gold

"Here at the Royal Institute of Alchemists we investigate everything, big and small. I foresee this invention will be invaluable to our research. Our current project is turning seawater into gold. This has received a lot of attention in recent months. Roger is one of our most eminent members and we fully intend to use his device to tell us if we have succeeded."

BUSTLING BRUGES GETS BOOST FROM NEW CRANE

The city of Bruges astonished the merchant world when it unveiled its revolutionary new crane. Running off a totally clean and renewable power source, it has been heralded as the way forward for all major trading ports.

"The mechanism is very simple," its operator explained. "There are two treadwheels. People get in them and walk on the spot. As the treadwheels turn, so the crane lifts the object."

Back to front

But workforce representatives are worried by this new mechanical device.

"This is all topsy-turvy," said one official. "If you took the people off the treadwheels and put them to work, they would do the job of loading and unloading cargoes just as efficiently as the crane."

Good eyeful

Port bosses dismissed such suggestions with an impatient shrug.

"How unimaginative. We foresee great things for this crane, particularly in the construction industry. Soon we will have gigantic versions of it, which will be able to lift much greater loads than mere humans.

"Not only that, the operator will sit at the top, and as the people below turn the treadwheel he will be able to swivel the crane so that he can see in everybody's bedroom windows. And when the nights are dark, at Christmas say, you could put bright lights on the crane. That would really brighten the place up."

A crane. Did the inventor keep pet hamsters?

BUSINESS NEWS

MERCHANT EMPIRE IN MONOPOLY CONTROVERSY

Baltic business "bullies" claim

The Hanseatic League, long one of Europe's biggest trading organizations, has defied the rules by cornering the market in all produce from the Baltic.

The German-based league is an extraordinary success story, with trading posts as far apart as Bruges, London and Novgorod in Russia.

It started out as a confederation of north German towns and merchant associations, selling **pickled Baltic herrings**. From there it expanded its operations to include **wheat, timber** and **amber**. It received valuable strongarm backing from the powerful Teutonic Knights, a less-than-holy order who have been creating **mayhem** in Poland and Prussia under the guise of mounting a crusade.

Mint

Before long the league was so powerful that it **minted its own coins**, which became solid currency in every European state.

To begin with, the league did much useful work, protecting trade from pirates and robbers, building lighthouses, and training pilots to guide its ships through dangerous waters.

But not everyone likes the league. Foreign merchants have complained that they've used **bribes and loans** to win valuable European trading contracts, and **excluded** merchants outside their organization from trading in the areas they operate in.

Even more outrageously, when top Dane King Valdemar IV decided that Denmark wanted a slice of Baltic trade the league defeated their navy, crushed their army and took over Denmark. They only left when the Danes agreed that league merchants could do whatever they liked wherever they wanted. (All signed sealed and delivered in the 1370 Peace of Stralsund, fact fans!)

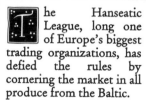

Business is booming for the Baltic-based Hanseatic League.

LOAVES IN NUMBER FIASCO

Bakers are furious at new legislation which says they must be honest. Instead of short-changing customers they are having to give them more than they asked for.

"The problem lies with bakers selling rolls in units of twelve," said a trading standards officer. "This means they can charge the same price whether the rolls are the size of a walnut or the size of footballs. We're introducing a new scheme whereby all rolls have to be a uniform weight. Officials will be touring the land making spot checks on suspect establishments. If they detect any knavery in

the ovens they will levy a massive fine and throw the offender into a rat-infested cell."

But bakers claim this is unfair as most of them don't have any scales and have to go by guesswork. As a spokesman from Consolidated Buns, the bakers' guild, pointed out, this is leading to massive overproduction.

"In many areas bakers live in fear for their lives. They're so scared they don't dare give customers 12 rolls any more. They give them 13, just in case they might be serving an inspector. This is disrupting the chain of production and baffling the population. It's an outrage."

A bakery yesterday. Support was not forthcoming from either the butchers or candlestick makers.

Messenger PERSONAL

Looking for Master or Mistress Right? Then start right here!!

Please send all replies to the *Messenger* office quoting the appropriate reference. Ads accepted at two groats per word. Boxed ads 20 groats per line. Please allow at least 12 months for any reply.

🌹 **PRINCESS,** 26, brunette, own teeth, would like to meet prince or similar, castle--and-keep type, aged around 30. Must have excellent prospects. BZ/1208

🌹 **BALDING,** pockmarked dung merchant would like to meet tall, blonde goddess with view to marriage. No time wasters please. BZ/2085

🌹 **ME Fulk.** You Jane. Hairy-chested crusader seeks lissom lass to join him in life's jungle. BZ/2096

🌹 **JINGLE** my bells! Court jester wants silly soulmate for days of endless japes, jokes and jollity. Sense of fun essential. BZ/2078

🌹 **CHIVALRIC** squire seeks married princess to worship from afar. Quite harmless. DL/3890

🌹 **LONELY** king, recently deposed, would like to meet similar queen. All letters answered. BZ/1901

🌹 **PROFESSIONAL** knight seeks dishy damsel. My interests include fighting, arson, fighting, murder, fighting, warfare, battles, sieges, fighting, chain-mail, fighting, weaponry, fighting, long walks and cozy evenings by the fire. What are yours? GQ/0001

🌹 **DESPERATELY** seeking Sibyl. Ex-monk Stephen seeks maiden to pamper and adore. Your portrait gets mine. FO/1242

🌹 **FOAMING AT MOUTH** Mongol-horde type guy, tired of looting and pillaging, seeks quiet Mrs. Mouse to snuggle up to in comfy little love nest. MH/149.

🌹 **WEALTHY** merchant (own fleet of trading vessels) seeks decorative lady for banquets and trade fairs. An ermine coat awaits! IC/498

🌹 **LOVE, HEALTH,** money, relation-ships – clairvoyant advises on all aspects of your life. No burners-at-the-stake please. RC/365

Miscellaneous

TYRANT seeks cowering populace. Impeccable qualifications – B.Sc. Tyranny, M.A. Mayhem, Hon. Fellow Genghis Khan School of Deportment. TM/134

FANCY a dose of viper pills, beaver kidneys or powdered clay? Druggist offers confidential treatment in your own home. Any area. Cleanliness and discretion assured and expected. BO/6579

BORED young mercenary looking for work. Major war preferred. But will accept a good uprising. In fact, will do anything for money. TM/176

ARE you a dragon or other imaginary beast? College of Heralds has constant demand for unusual animals. Apply in writing in first instance. TP/2002

MAGNUS of Pomerania. Please send another letter. Your last was accidentally eaten during a terrible famine. BZ/1166

IS there anybody out there? Map-maker, 32, financially secure, would like to hear from anything and anybody who lives beyond the known bounds of geography. OT/658

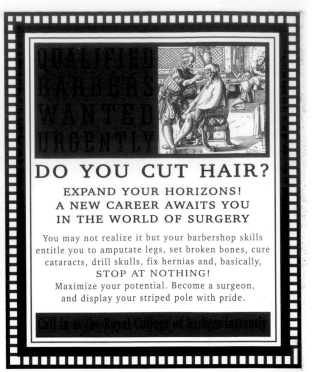

SPOT THE DIFFERENCE

How observant are you? Test your prowess with these two pictures of merry dancing peasants.

Picture 1 shows them dancing to the sound of a skirling bagpipe. Picture 2 shows the same scene, but with a few subtle differences. There are ten in all. See if you can spot them!

1

2

Win a pilgrimage for two!... Win a pilgrimage for two!... Win a pilgrimage for two!... Win a pilgrimage for two!...

YES! IT'S VISORS DOWN FOR...
SPOT THE BATTLE AXE!

For this week's competition we've chosen a picture of a rollicking, hands-on, heads-off, punch-up. Study the picture closely and use your skill and judgement to spot the battle axe. It's in there somewhere!

CLUE: It's a long stick with two pieces of curved metal on the end.

The lucky winner gets two tickets for the pilgrimage of his or her choice.*

Last week's winner was Enid Shrub of Rive Gauche, Paris. She receives a brand new layer of earth for her living-room floor. Congratulations Enid!

*The word chooses is used here in a purely imaginary fashion and is not meant to suggest any site of religious interest beyond the immediate locality of the winner's home.

BALDRICS
HOME STORES
MAIL-ORDER BROCHURE

As we approach the 50th season of the 100 Years War, BALDRICS is offering super-special goods at super-silly prices. Here are just a few of our crazy anniversary bargains.

PROTECTION

MACE. Not the spice but the genuine article. Muggers will run a mile when they see you. 1 DUCAT.

WOOLLIES

HOSE. A must for every peasant. Pre-grovelled for extra comfort. SIXPENCE.

MILITARY WARE

FULL METAL JACKET, trousers, shoes and gloves. Our stylish battle-dress looks as good in the pub as it does on the battlefield. Extra reinforcement at wrists and elbows to protect those valuable drinking joints. Helmet comes down to neck level, with closeable visor to shut out unwanted bar chatter. Perfect for a knight on the tiles! 7 DUCATS!

LATEST FASHIONS

CAPE AND COWL. Who would have thought it! At last a quality garment which combines practical-ity with anonymity. Made from best English wool, this head-to-toe outfit keeps the elements at bay while obscuring your iden-tity from friend and foe alike. Watch expressions change from dread to delight as you fling back the hood to reveal that you are not the Angel of Death. 2 FLORINS.

HAIR CARE

SNOOD. Too much hair? This delightful hat comes with a bag attached. Just right for storing those excess tresses. ONLY 15 GROATS!

WINCH WARE

GET BACK IN THE SADDLE with a Williams winch. Are you one of those knights who just can't get on his horse when he wants to? It's noisy, painful and embarrassing. AND IT ALWAYS HAPPENS WHEN YOU'RE IN A HURRY! Williams Winches have designed a winch which is tailor-made for you. Just step into the loops and give your squire the signal. NO PROBLEMS. NO FUSS. As used by the flower of chivalry. ONLY 5 DUCATS.

EXCLUSIVE HEADWEAR

WIMPLE. A snood for the more mature lady. Completely covers the head, leaving only the face on view. No one need know how little hair you have. (Priory discounts are available for nuns.) 10 GROATS!

QUALITY FOOTWEAR

SILLY SHOES. We don't know why no one has thought of good, leather boots. But until they do we shall continue to stock these pointy things. Shows off the one-toed foot to perfection. 9 FLORINS!

With every order please add 3 groats for ox-and-cartage.

There is only one
BALDRICS
There is only one sale

Remember, with our unique, no-quibbles, groats-back guarantee, you can buy in confidence from BALDRICS.

PICTURE CREDITS: © akg-images p12 mr Erich Lessing, p28 br De Agostini Picture Lib.; © Alamy p4 m © Sonia Halliday Photographs, p10 br © Holmes Garden Photos/Alamy Stock Photo; © The Art Archive p6 Victoria and Albert Museum London/V&A Images; p8 tr Bodleian Libraries, Bodley 264 folio 231v, The University of Oxford, p15 ml Bodleian Libraries, The University of Oxford/Bodley 764 folio 63r, p27 t University Library Heidelberg/Collection Dagli Orti, p29 tl Hamburg Staatsarchiv/Harper Collins Publishers; © Bridgeman Images Cover t © British Library Board. All Rights Reserved, cover mr © Lambeth Palace Library, London, UK, p1 © British Library Board. All Rights Reserved, p2 tr © British Library Board. All Rights Reserved, p3 t Musée de la Tapisserie, Bayeux, France/With special authorisation of the city of Bayeux, br © British Library Board. All Rights Reserved, p4 bl Bibliotheque Nationale, Paris, France, p5 tl © British Library Board. All Rights Reserved, br Bibliotheque Nationale, Paris, France, p7 tr © Prado, Madrid, Spain, p8 mr Attila the Hun (woodcut), Anonymous/Private Collection, p18 tl © British Library Board. All Rights Reserved, ml © British Library Board. All Rights Reserved, p19 tr Bibliotheque Nationale, Paris, France, p21 br © British Library Board. All Rights Reserved, p23 br © British Library Board. All Rights Reserved, p24 tr © British Library Board. All Rights Reserved, mr © British Library Board. All Rights Reserved, p29 b © British Library Board. All Rights Reserved, p30 br © British Library Board. All Rights Reserved, p31 br Bibliotheque Nationale, Paris, France, © The British Library Board p21 l Harley 5762 f 62, p25 tr Harley 4425 f.166, p26 br Harley MS 4751 f 36r; © Corbis cover bl; © Topfoto Grainger Collection p7br, p16; © Mary Evans Picture Library p8 m © Photo Researchers, p28 m, p30 tr INTERFOTO/Sammlung Rauch; Photo © RMN p18 mr Grand Palais (domaine de Chantilly)/René-Gabriel Ojéda, p22 BnF, Dist. RMN-Grand Palais/image BnF, p23 tm Grand Palais (domaine de Chantilly)/René-Gabriel Ojéda, p30 tm Grand Palais (domaine de Chantilly)/René-Gabriel Ojéda; Courtesy Temple Church London p6b Photo Brian Voakes.